The Big Game

Written by Louise A. Gikow

Illustrated by Phil Garner

My First
READER

children's press®

A Division of Scholastic Inc.
New York Toronto London Auckland Sydney
Mexico City New Delhi Hong Kong
Danbury, Connecticut

Library of Congress Cataloging-in-Publication Data

Gikow, Louise.
  The big game / written by Louise A. Gikow ; illustrated by Phil Garner.
      p. cm. – (My first reader)
  ISBN 0-516-24408-6 (lib. bdg.)   0-516-25500-2 (pbk.)
  [1. Soccer–Fiction. 2. Individuality–Fiction. 3. Stories in rhyme.]
I. Garner, Phil, 1961- ill. II. Title. III. Series.
  PZ8.3.G376Bi 2004
  [E]–dc22
                                2003014068

12 13 14 15 R 20 19 18 17   62

Scholastic Inc., 557 Broadway, New York, NY 10012.

Note to Parents and Teachers

Once a reader can recognize and identify the 43 words used to tell this story, he or she will be able to successfully read the entire book. These 43 words are repeated throughout the story, so that young readers will be able to recognize the words easily and understand their meaning.

The 43 words used in this book are:

all	he	meet	there
at	he's	on	to
ball	hooray	play	today
can	if	plays	too
cannot	is	run	way
day	it	soccer	we
do	its	something	what
every	José	stop	why
fun	kick	stopped	win
good	knows	that	you
having	likes	the	

Meet José. He likes to play.

He plays soccer every day.

José cannot kick at all.

He cannot kick the soccer ball.

He cannot kick. He cannot run.

Why is José having fun?

There is something he can do.

José knows that he's good, too.

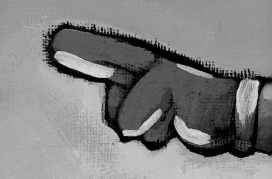

He knows what to do today.

Can you stop the ball, José?

The soccer ball is on its way.

Stop it! Stop the ball, José!

If you do, we win today!

You stopped the ball! Hooray, José!

ABOUT THE AUTHOR

Louise A. Gikow has written hundreds of books for children (and a few for young adults and grown-ups, too). She wrote *The Big Game* because she loves soccer, and she's glad it's become so popular with kids these days. Gikow has also written songs and scripts for videos and television shows. Most recently, she was a writer for *Between the Lions,* the PBS-Kids TV series that helps children learn to read.

ABOUT THE ILLUSTRATOR

Phil Garner has been an illustrator for more than fifteen years. He's drawn and painted loads of interesting things, from pirates and clowns to ghosts and robots and everything in between. Garner lives in England. He likes sports and plays soccer but, unlike José, he's not a very good goalie.